Bradwell's
Family Cycle Rides
The Peak District

BRADWELL'S
FAMILY CYCLE RIDES
THE PEAK DISTRICT

PAUL FRANCIS COOPER

BRADWELL
BOOKS

Published by Bradwell Books

9 Orgreave Close Sheffield S13 9NP

Email: books@bradwellbooks.co.uk

1st Edition

ISBN: 9781910551868

Design by: Mark Titterton

Typesetting and Mapping: Mark Titterton

Photograph Credits: Photographs © Paul Francis Cooper
p.7, p.28, p.31-top, p.48, p.78, p.82-both, p.85 © Mark Titterton

p.80-81 iStock

Print: CPI Group (UK) Ltd, Croydon, CR0 4YY

Maps: Contain Ordnance Survey data

© Crown copyright and database right 2017

Ordnance Survey licence number 100039353

The information in this book has been produced in good faith and is intended as a general guide. Although the maps in this book are based on original Ordnance Survey (OS) mapping, cyclists are always advised to use a detailed OS map. Look in 'The Basics' section for recommendations for the most suitable map for each of the rides.

Bradwell Books and the author have made all reasonable efforts to ensure that the details are correct at the time of publication. Bradwell Books and the author cannot accept responsibility for any changes that have taken place subsequent to the book being published.

It is the responsibility of individuals undertaking any of the cycle rides listed in this book to exercise due care and consideration for their own health and wellbeing and that of others in their party. Most of the routes in this book are not especially strenuous, but individuals taking part should ensure they are fit and well before setting off.

A well-maintained bicycle is essential for these rides but no specialist equipment is necessary (see 'Equipment' in the introduction). It is advisable but not essential to wear cycling-specific clothing as this will make you more comfortable, and don't forget to take a waterproof in case of rain. Because the rides will take some time, it would be a good idea to take along some food and drink.

Enjoy cycling in the Peak District with Bradwell Books!

CONTENTS

Introduction   6

1. Alsop-en-le-Dale (Moderate) 8¾ miles / 14km   10

2. Carsington Water (Easy) 8 miles / 13km   14

3. Derwent Reservoir (Moderate) 11 miles / 18km   18

4. Ladybower Reservoir (Easy – Moderate) 5½ miles / 9km   24

5. Hartington, Biggin and Parsley Hay (Moderate) 8½miles / 13.5km   26

6. High Peak Trail (Moderate) 24 miles / 38km   32

7. Hulme End, Wetton and Wetton Mill (Moderate) 8 miles / 13km   36

8. Hulme End, Alstonefield and Milldale (Moderate) 9 miles / 14.5km   40

9. Ilam, Throwley, Waterhouses, Manifold Way, Tissington Trail   44
    and Thorpe (Difficult) 30 miles / 48km

10. Ilam, Blore, Mapleton and Thorpe (Difficult) 7 miles / 11km   50

11. Longdendale Trail (Moderate) 13 miles / 21km   54

12. Manifold Way (Easy) 18 miles / 29km   58

13. Monsal Trail (Easy) 9 miles / 14km   64

14. Sett Valley Trail (Easy) 5 miles / 8km   70

15. Tissington Trail: Ashbourne – Parsley Hay and return (Easy) 26 miles / 42km 74

16. Tissington, Bradbourne and Carsington Water (Moderate) 9½ miles / 14km 82

17. Tissington, Parsley Hay, Hartington Station, Harding's Lane and   86
    Liff's Road (Moderate) 20 miles / 32km

18. Wye Dale, Monsal Trail and Millers Dale (Moderate) 8¾ miles / 14km   92

About the Author   96

Easy rides on trails will be fine for riders who have yet to develop their competence in bike handling and in riding on public roads.

Moderate rides will require competence on public roads and a readiness to give some climbing and descending a go.

Difficult rides require proficiency in bike-handling and road-riding competence as well as the stamina to cope over varying distances, which include hill-climbing and descents.

INTRODUCTION

CYCLING IN THE PEAK DISTRICT

The Peak District's rolling landscape, with its reservoirs, lakes and rivers, miles of quiet country lanes and historic villages is a natural destination for any cyclist. And, for family cyclists, its 65 miles of traffic-free trails make it especially attractive.

This book guides family cyclists along the trails and suggests some rides for those who want to branch out from them to the lanes and climbs of the area.

DIFFICULTY GRADINGS

Each ride is provided with an assessment of the difficulty level of the ride – easy, moderate, or difficult. This has been gauged with the ability levels of family cyclists in mind and takes account of distance, the amount of climbing and descending and any technical demands, for example, road surfaces or sharp bends. Easy rides on trails will be fine for riders who have yet to develop their competence in bike handling and in riding on public roads. Moderate rides will require competence on public roads and a readiness to give some climbing and descending a go. Difficult rides require proficiency in bike-handling and road-riding competence as well as the stamina to cope over varying distances, which include hill-climbing and descents.

DURATION OF RIDE

This depends on a number of factors, which include riders' ability levels, stops for sightseeing and refreshments, and, on the more difficult rides, the amount of climbing involved. The time estimates in the book are generous, but are meant only as a rough guide. Once you've done a couple of rides you'll start to get a better idea of your own particular pace and how quickly you want to travel.

EQUIPMENT

As long as your bike is in sound working order and you take account of the following information, you won't need any specialist riding equipment for these rides.

TYRES

Since most of the rides in the book take you, at least for some of the time, on to trails, you'll need solid tyres with puncture protection. There's no such thing as a puncture-proof tyre, but ones with Vectran or Kevlar breaker layers will cope well with the sort of gritty and uneven surfaces that you may well meet. While heavy-duty mountain bike tyres aren't necessary – and may actually create unnecessary resistance on tarmac – wider tyres do give greater protection on uneven terrain. Medium width, say 28–33cm (subject to clearance on your bike frames) should be ideal. This will give the right off-road grip but won't slow you down too much if you want to be a bit more adventurous on tarmac. Finally,

remember to inflate the tyre to the recommended level as indicated on the tyre wall. This reduces surface resistance and helps to prevent punctures.

With any luck these measures should keep you puncture-free, but you can never be assured of that happy state. So make sure that at least one member of your group can change an inner tube, pack a spare tube on each bike, and have at least one pump and a pair of tyre levers on hand for the ride.

GEARS

Gradients on the trails are not particularly severe – most are converted railway tracks – so it's perfectly possible to ride the trails without a large number of gears. Out on the lanes, though, you will encounter some climbs, and so a good choice of gears is strongly advised. They're not essential, though, if you remember that, if a climb is too difficult, there is always the option of getting off the bike and pushing your way to the top – a rule that applies no matter how many gears your bike has!

BIKE SECURITY

Always remember to lock your bike to something solid if you leave it unattended. There are a number of times on these rides when you'll want to leave your bike to do a little on-foot exploring. The Peak District doesn't have a particularly troubling crime rate but nobody's told bike thieves that.

CLOTHING

Cycling-specific clothing, such as Lycra shorts, leggings and cycling jerseys with rear pockets is designed for comfort and practicality on longer rides – the value of chamois padding in shorts is inestimable on a long day in the saddle. But they are not essential for the rides in this book. In warmer weather, trail shorts and T-shirts, or on cooler days, jeans and lightweight, breathable, jackets will be fine. (It's also possible to buy padded underwear to ease the risk of saddle soreness).

Whatever you choose to wear, always be sure to have a waterproof top with you. The weather in the Peak District can be changeable and the undoubted joys of two-wheeled travel fade very quickly when you become cold and wet.

GOOD CYCLISTS CODE

1. Keep to the left and be respectful to other users.
2. Please use your bell or give a warning so that other trail users know you are approaching.
3. On no account should you race along the trails.
4. Only designated routes should be used.

1 ALSOP-EN-LE-DALE, TISSINGTON, PARWICH, ALSOP-EN-LE-DALE

If you like quiet lanes amid gentle pasture land, unspoilt villages and historic country churches, this circular ride will suit you. From Alsop-en-le-dale Station car park, the site of the old village station, it takes you along the Tissington Trail and then, on quiet lanes, through three picturesque Peak District villages.

In cycling, as in life, there's rarely such a thing as a free lunch, so be prepared: the ride does have a couple of short, steep climbs. But, with a couple of short pushes of the bike, one of them up a steep footpath, these manageable exertions are a price well worth paying for an enjoyable morning or afternoon in picture-perfect countryside.

The ride starts with a gentle three-mile descent along the Tissington Trail to Tissington village. You need to leave the trail here, and you will be well rewarded if, when you do, you spend some time in the village. It's a popular and well-visited location and with good reason. With a duck pond, a 12th-century church and a Jacobean hall, home to the FitzHerbert family, owners of the Tissington Estate since the reign of Elizabeth I, it makes for a pleasant early break to your ride.

Peaceful as Tissington is today, its history is rich in Britain's warlike past. The village was a site for an English Civil War skirmish between parliamentarian and royalist forces, who were supported by the FitzHerberts. If you look closely at the pillars to the Norman doorway of St Mary's Church you'll see marks in the stonework. These grooves were carved by the young men of the village and surrounding area as they sharpened their arrows for archery practice to be ready for calls to military service.

It's back on your bikes for a mile or so as your route takes you through the open pastureland of the Tissington Estate before a short descent to another feature of the ride, Tissington Ford. It makes for an interesting crossing of Bradbourne Brook. It's not often that you'll cross a ford in your travels in the UK today, but don't worry, there's a footbridge for pedestrians and cyclists to make a safe and dry crossing.

Your next village stop is Parwich. This quiet, unassuming home to no more than 500 people acquired national status when the Sunday Times named it one of the best places to live in Britain. You may well agree. It has two village ponds, a village green, Georgian, limestone cottages, and the centre-piece church of St Peter. Although it was substantially rebuilt in the 19th century, St Peter's traces its roots to the Normans.

The ride finally takes you to the peaceful hamlet of Alsop-en-le-Dale. If you pause at the hamlet's church of St Michael and All

Angels, you'll see zig-zag patterned mouldings over its doorway, a sure sign of another church with Norman origins. Enjoy a few quiet moments in the churchyard overlooked by the Tissington Trail, then head for your return point, which is up a nearby steep footpath to the site of the old railway station where you started.

THE BASICS

Distance: 8¾ miles / 14 km

Gradient: Mostly flat, but the ride includes a gentle descent and a number of short but sharp climbs

Severity: Moderate

Approx. time: 3 hours

Terrain: Well-surfaced cycle trail and tarmac lanes. Public roads are quiet, but riders must be competent to ride on open roads

Maps: OS Explorer OL 24 or OS Landranger 119

Start point: Alsop-en-le-Dale Station (GR: SK 156548)

Parking: Alsop-en-le-Dale Station car park (nearest postcode: DE6 1QP)

Public toilets: Alsop-en-le-Dale Station car park, Tissington Station car park

Nearest food: Tissington village

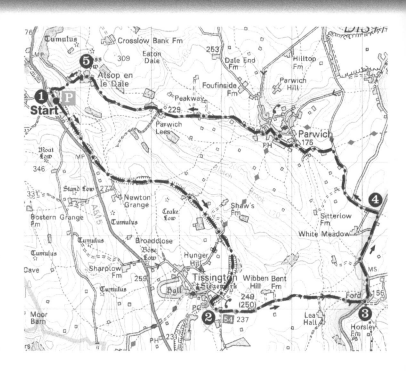

DIRECTIONS

1. Join the Tissington Trail from the car park at Alsop-en-le-Dale Station and head south along the trail to Tissington Village Station.

2.   Leave the trail at the site of the old station pass through the car park turn right to enter Tissington village.

After visiting the village retrace your ride as though rejoining the trail. Instead of turning right into the car park you carry on along Darfield and then continue onto Bent Lane.

Follow the lanes for approximately one mile until your descent to Bradbourne Brook and Tissington Ford.

At the ford dismount to take the footpath and footbridge over the ford and then make the very short climb to the junction of the B5056.

3.   At the junction turn left and follow the B5056 for approximately one mile where you will see a signpost for Ballidon and Parwich.

4.   Turn left and continue along the mildly undulating and winding road until you reach the village of Parwich. As you do, you'll see a sign and milepost for Alsop-en-le-Dale (2 miles) and Newhaven (4 miles). Take some time to explore Parwich, then retrace your route to continue on the road  towards Alsop-en-le-Dale. You'll climb sharply at times, but the road levels in approximately 2 miles as it nears the hamlet of Alsop-en-le-Dale.

5.   A short distance after St Michael and All Angels church you should spot a footpath on your left. Dismount to make the short hike – ascending quite sharply – to rejoin the Tissington Trail at your start point, Alsop-en-le-Dale Station.

Excellent, outdoor recreation that it is, there are days when you need something more than a bike ride for your family day out. When that happens Carsington Water fits the bill.

As well as its eight-mile cycle circuit of the lake, there is an extensive visitor centre, cafe, watersports facility, nature reserves, a children's playground, and a chance to sit and relax at the lakeside – all within a setting of some very enjoyable scenery.

The lake is a man-made reservoir, which, with a capacity of 7,800 million gallons of water, is the ninth biggest reservoir in the UK. Run by Severn Trent Water Authority, it was opened by The Queen in 1992 and it supplies homes in Nottinghamshire, Derbyshire and Leicestershire. Plans for a reservoir at Carsington were first developed in the 1960s but, given its scale, the project had to clear two public inquiries before work could start in 1979.

During its construction four workers tragically lost their lives in what is now known as the Carsington Incident. Carbon dioxide seeped from surrounding limestone into an inspection chamber where the men were working and fatally depleted their oxygen supplies. Excavations during the lake's construction discovered Roman remains and archaeologists think that Carsington was known in Roman times as Lutudarum, a centre

for the Roman lead industry. Now it's an excellent destination for a day out, hosting more than one million visitors each year.

The cycle trail runs close to the lakeside and, throughout its eight miles, cuts through deep woodland and open pasture offering plenty of views of the lake. The surface is good and, though there are plenty of ups and downs along the way, there are no long, or particularly steep, climbs to over-tire young legs. The route also has some sharp turns but these are well signposted and, with a little adult caution, are easily dealt with.

Navigation is straightforward. It's just a question of following the trail signposting, which directs you throughout. The choice of direction – clockwise or anti-clockwise, starting from the visitor centre – is up to you, although it's worth remembering that the anti-clockwise route probably offers a better view along the dam wall to the visitor centre – a worthy curtain call to the final stages of your ride.

THE BASICS

Distance: 8 miles / 13km

Gradient: Some short climbs and descents with undulation throughout the ride

Severity: Easy

Approx. time: 2 hours

Terrain: Well-surfaced trail. The trail goes through woodland and fields, which are used for open cattle grazing. There are a number of gates to open and close

Maps: OS Explorer OL 24 or OS Landranger 119

Start point: Carsington Water Visitor Centre (GR: SK 241516)

Parking: Adjacent to Visitor Centre (postcode: DE6 1ST)

Public toilets: Carsington Water Visitor Centre

Nearest food: Carsington Water Visitor Centre

DIRECTIONS

Clear and frequent signposting starts at the information board directly in front of the visitor centre. There is a choice between clockwise and anti-clockwise routes.

INTRODUCTION TO RIDE 3 AND 4

It's little wonder that the Upper Derwent Valley is one of the most popular Peak District destinations for leisure cyclists. Two accessible trails, cutting through dense woodland, run along the valley's sides above Howden,  Derwent and Ladybower reservoirs. On one side, the valley drops steeply away from the trails to the deep, dark reservoirs, and on the other it rises to the valley ridge and the surrounding, heather-covered moors.

Both trails are circuits, much of which are traffic-free, and where there is traffic it is limited. The trails start and finish at the valley's 'Fairholmes' visitor centre, where there is a bike hire and cycle repair shop and a friendly cafe. Family cyclists have a choice of rides and can be sure that a day out in the Upper Derwent Valley will meet their needs.

3 DERWENT AND HOWDEN RESERVOIR TRAIL

The most demanding ride involves the longer pedal around the Howden and Derwent reservoirs. This includes a steady climb and a strenuous stretch on a bridleway. The shorter ride skirts the Ladybower Reservoir and follows a cycle lane over the Ashopton Viaduct which spans the Ladybower Reservoirs. This ride includes a comfortable descent on a well-surfaced trail and a steady return climb on a tarmac road. And, of course, there is the option of combining both rides to make one long circuit.

No matter which ride you prefer, you'll experience a dramatic and sweeping landscape. The valley is a haven for birdlife, and, if you're very lucky, you may spot one of the goshawks, now a rare breed, who have made the Upper Derwent their home.

The valley is also rich in history. Plans were made at the end of the 19th century to meet the need for clean water in the growing cities of Sheffield, Leicester, Derby and Nottingham. Following an Act of Parliament, the Derwent and Howden Dams were built between 1901 and 1916. The valley was then so isolated, and the building project so great, that a corrugated iron village, officially called Birchinlee, but nicknamed 'Tin Town', housed the workers who built the huge dams out of 1.2 million tons of locally quarried stone. You'll pass the site of the village if you make the climb to the head of Howden reservoir where the Slippery Stones Bridge crosses the River Derwent.

The Upper Derwent and Howden reservoirs changed the physical landscape of the valley for ever. But upheaval of another form was to follow when Ladybower Reservoir was subsequently built. Opened by King George VI in September 1945, its design involved a controversial plan to flood two of the valley's villages, Derwent and Ashopton.

Ashopton's remains are totally submerged under the Ladybower Reservoir, but in dry summers, when the water level recedes, it's possible, when cycling around the Derwent Reservoir, to spot some of the flooded buildings of Derwent – the sad, last remnants of the Peak District village. Well, not quite the last: nearby Jubilee Cottages, sitting above the high water mark, survived, as did the Slippery Stones Bridge, which now crosses the

Derwent at the head of the Howden Reservoir. It was once the medieval packhorse bridge in Derwent village, and, being subject to a preservation order, it was moved to its current location. High above its historic, original surroundings, it was rebuilt, stone by stone, before its former village home was flooded.

Another historic feature of the valley is its link with the famous Second World War RAF 617 (Dambusters) Squadron. Because of the physical similarity to the squadron's secret targets – the Möhne and Edersee dams of the Ruhr Valley – air crews flew their Lancaster bombers repeatedly over Howden and Upper Derwent Reservoirs as they prepared meticulously for their dangerous, low-level raid. There is a small museum to the squadron and its links with the valley (open on Sundays) in the West Tower of the Derwent dam.

For riders with a bit more stamina, then why not join these two rides together?

THE BASICS

Distance: 11 miles / 18km

Gradient: Demanding, steady climb with comfortable descent on return leg

Severity: Moderate

Approx. time: 2 hours

Terrain: Tarmac roads and bridleway

Maps: OS Explorer or OS Landranger 110

Start point: Fairholmes Visitor Centre (GR: SK 172893)

Parking: Fairholmes Visitor Centre, pay and display (nearest postcode: S33 0AQ). On Sundays throughout the year and on Saturdays and Bank Holidays from Easter to October the road beyond Fairholmes Visitor Centre is closed to motor vehicles. A roundabout exists at the entrance to the visitor centre with a sign indicating when full parking capacity has been reached. At peak times in summer months it may not be possible to park at the centre. It is possible to park further down the valley in parking spaces off the Lower Derwent Reservoir road

Public toilets: Fairholmes Visitor Centre

Nearest food: Fairholmes Visitor Centre

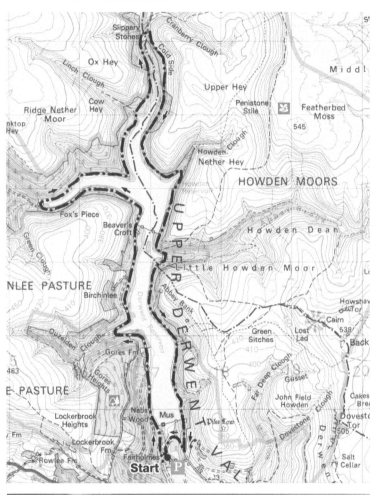

DIRECTIONS

Fairholmes Visitor Centre, West Bank of Upper Derwent and Howden Reservoirs, crossing Slippery Stones, returning via East Bank

1. Leave the cycle hire centre behind you following the one-way road to the exit of the centre at the T-junction.

2. Turn sharp right.

3. Follow the road for approximately 6 miles. This involves a steady climb until you reach a turning point.

4. At the turning point leave the road and enter the bridleway via the farm gate.

5. Follow the bridleway, which is signposted for Slippery Stones, until you reach the Slippery Stones Bridge.

6. After crossing the bridge, turn slight right to continue on the bridleway until you reach the farm gate to the reservoir road.

7. Continue for approximately 4½ miles. The road involves a steady descent with glimpses of the reservoirs through the trees on your right.

8. At 4½ miles turn sharp right in the direction of the Derwent Dam.

9. Continue for approximately ½ miles, crossing the dam wall to arrive back at Fairholmes Visitor Centre.

THE BASICS

Distance: 5½ miles / 9km

Gradient: Steady descent to Ashopton Viaduct, steady return climb

Severity: Easy to Moderate

Approx. time: 1 to 1½ Hours

Terrain: Well-surfaced trail and tarmac road surface

Maps: OS Explorer OL1 or OS Landranger 110

Start point: Fairholmes Visitor Centre (GR: SK 172893)

Parking: Fairholmes Visitor Centre, pay and display (nearest postcode: S33 0AQ) See note on page 21 about seasonal parking

Public toilets: Fairholmes Visitor Centre

Nearest food: Fairholmes Visitor Centre

DIRECTIONS

Fairholmes Visitor Centre via Derwent Lane to Ashopton Viaduct

1. Leaving the visitor centre, cross the Derwent dam wall.

2. Join Derwent Lane and continue with a steady descent for approximately 2½ miles.

3. At the junction of the Snake Pass (A57) turn sharp right, taking the safe cycle lane across the Ashopton Viaduct.

4. At the end of the viaduct turn sharp right.

5. Make the steady climb up the tarmac road for approximately 2½ miles to the roundabout, which is the entrance to Fairholmes Visitor Centre.

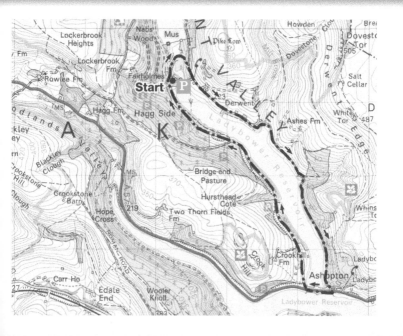

This easy circuit ride may not be long – starting and finishing in the historic village of Hartington, it's only seven miles in total. But you'll be more than satisfied with what you cover in those miles.

The ride includes quiet country lanes, an open stretch of the Tissington Trail, a cafe stop with great views of the surrounding countryside, and a home-run descent through dramatic limestone crags. The ride is suitable for adults, young people and children who are competent riding beyond cycle trails and who can manage a steady descent on a quiet lane.

Hartington is an ideal start and finish point. It has a number of cafes, one of which is the 17th-century Hartington Hall. An impressive Elizabethan-style building, the story has it that Bonnie Prince Charlie stayed here in December 1745 during the southern advance of his highland army in the ill-fated Jacobite Rising. The village gained a market charter from King John in 1203, one of the earliest market charters in the area. And its spacious square, with its fine buildings surrounding a large duck pond, is evidence of how it prospered as a result. Its duck pond, though, has links with the darkness of medieval times. Women judged to be gossips or 'scolds' were once submerged in its cold water in a ducking stool and nearby stood a set of gallows.

St Giles' Church stands in a proud position above the village square and is probably the only medieval building remaining in Hartington. Most of the building dates from the 13th and 14th centuries with extensive, but sensitive, 19th-century restoration.

A steady two-mile climb from the village will get you to the site of the old Hartington railway station on the Buxton to Ashbourne line. In common with other old stations on the line, now the Tissington Trail, nothing remains of the station itself. (The site houses a car park, toilets and an entrance to the trail.) Delightfully preserved, though, is the station signal box. Visible high above the approaching road it provides an attractive and colourful landmark for the trail.

The two-mile ride along the trail, embanked high above the surrounding countryside, leads you to the welcome sight of Parsley Hay Cycle Hire Centre, whose location is second to none. In addition to cycle hire facilities, you can enjoy the cafe's outdoor seating where you can relax and enjoy the views of the White Peak landscape. From there the ride makes a gentle descent back to Hartington along a quiet lane banked on both sides by dramatic limestone crags.

(An alternative starting point for this circuit ride is Parsley Hay Cycle Hire Centre if you are planning to hire a bike for your ride.)

THE BASICS

Distance: 8½ miles / 13.5km

Gradient: Steady climb for 2 miles from Hartington Village to Hartington Signal Box, flat along Tissington Trail, steady return descent

Severity: Moderate

Approx. time: 2 hours

Terrain: Tarmac roads, crushed limestone on Tissington Trail. Public roads have low levels of traffic. Tissington Trail is only accessible to cyclists and pedestrians

Maps: OS Explorer 24 or OS Landranger 119

Start point: Hartington Village duck pond, Dig Street (GR: SK 127604)

Parking: On low demand days free parking spaces are available in Dig Street (nearest postcode: SK17 0AH). Pay and display nearby at Parson's Field Mill Lane

Public toilets: Hartington village, Hartington Station, Parsley Hay

Nearest food: Hartington village, Parsley Hay Cafe

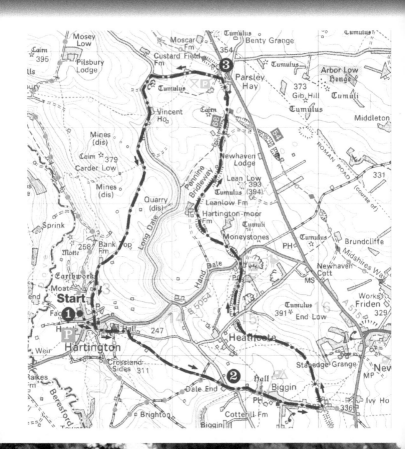

DIRECTIONS

1. Start at the duck pond in Hartington village. With the duck pond behind you and St Giles' Church on your left, turn left to briefly (60 metres) join the B5054. Turn right onto Hall Bank and follow for 500 metres. Then turn right onto Highfield Lane, follow this for 1 mile / 1.5km.

2. At the junction turn right and then left to Biggin, after 1 mile / 1.5km you can pick up the Tissington Trail by passing under a bridge, and turning immediately left up a ramp and then right once you join the trail.
Follow the trail for 3½ miles / 5.5km past Hartington Station Signal Box and on to Parsley Hay.

3. Take the ramp down from the cafe and turn right. Follow the lane for approximately ¾ miles until you meet a T-junction with Hide Lane.

4. Turn left and follow Hide Lane for approximately 3 miles until you meet a T-junction with the B5054.
Turn right and ride for approximately 300 metres to Hartington village square. The duck pond is to your right.

This 24-mile ride along the High Peak Trail, which runs from Middleton Top Visitor Centre to Parsley Hay Cycle Hire Centre and back again, gives you views across rugged hills, open pastures and woodland, and the opportunity to explore a wealth of wildflower.

As you'd expect from its name, the ride is more exposed than trails such as Tissington and Manifold. It's also more hilly with more twists and turns – great for varying your viewpoint, but overall tougher on your stamina. But there's nothing here that should deter any family cyclist, particularly since, as with any trail ride, there are plenty of opportunities to shorten the trip if the going starts to feel a bit tough.

Riding the High Peak Trail, bordered by dry limestone walls, rolling hills and remote sheep farms, it might not be easy to see a link with the birth of Britain's industrial age. But it's there. The trail runs on the trackbed of the old Cromford and High Peak Railway. Built between 1825 and 1830 it was one of the most improbable and bold civil engineering achievements of the Industrial Revolution and one of the first railways in the world.

It was built to link the Peak Forest Canal at Whaley Bridge (north of Buxton) to the Cromford Canal, a north–south journey of some 33 miles. On its flat stretches, much in the way of canal barges, it relied on horses to pull its wagons, while on its steep sections engine houses stored winding engines and special winding gear to do the job. It was bold, truly innovative and imaginative, but by today's standards it wasn't fast. In its earliest days the full 33-mile journey took two days. You'll make a much faster pace on your bike – even allowing for stops to savour remnants of Britain's Industrial Revolution in this wonderfully wild hilltop setting.

A good starting point for the return ride to Parsley Hay (always good for a cafe stop and turning point) is Middleton Top Visitor Centre. Parking, cycle hire and toilet facilities are there, and nearby Middleton Top Engine House, perched at the top of Middleton Incline, is a fascinating and well-maintained historical site. The 1829 beam engine, once used to wind the railway's wagons up the 1-in-8 gradient, is inside the engine house. You can see it in operation on the first weekend of each month in summer and on bank holidays. One of the wagons used on the line until it closed in 1963 is also there.

The ride from Middleton Top takes you through limestone gorges and the long, atmospheric Hopton Tunnel. Stop your bike and linger in the tunnel and you can almost hear the clank of the bygone, limestone-laden goods wagons. Out of the tunnel and it's

not long before you hit the long, steady ascent of Hopton Incline. It's not 1 in 8 but it's still steep enough for some riders to get off and walk. From there the trail levels for a rewarding ride to Parsley Hay and, of course, the delight of a return leg with a welcome downhill finish.

As with any trail there is always the option of stopping and turning. An interesting short route (which includes a ride through Hopton Tunnel) would be from Middleton Top to Harborough Rocks and back. It's a distance of about five miles in all. Sitting on a high ridge above Brassington, the rocks have long been a haunt of climbers and are easily accessible from the trail. In the early 18th century Daniel Defoe passed the rocks on his 'Tour Through the Whole Island of Great Britain'. There he found a family living in Harborough Cave, a natural cavern in the rocks. Archaeologists have since discovered evidence of people living in the cave in the Ice Age.

THE BASICS

Distance: 24 miles / 38km

Gradient: A slightly demanding ascent in the earlier stages of the outward ride, but the incline is in your favour on the return leg

Severity: Moderate

Approx. time: 2 to 3 hours

Terrain: Well-surfaced traffic-free cycle trail (two gated crossings of public roads en route should be approached with care) (DSC 9068)

Maps: OS Explorer OL 24 or OS Landranger 119

Start point: Middleton Top Visitor Centre (GR: SK 275551)

Parking: Near the visitor centre (nearest postcode: DE4 4LS)

Nearest food: Middleton Top Visitor Centre, Parsley Hay Cycle Hire Centre and Cafe

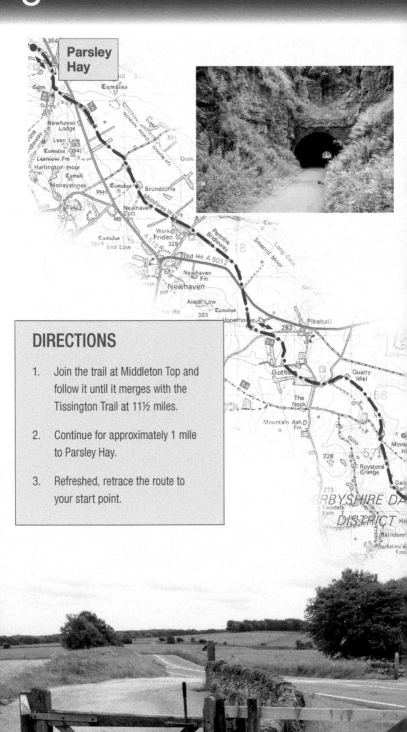

DIRECTIONS

1. Join the trail at Middleton Top and follow it until it merges with the Tissington Trail at 11½ miles.

2. Continue for approximately 1 mile to Parsley Hay.

3. Refreshed, retrace the route to your start point.

Middleton Top

Start

This eight-mile ride, starting from the old Hulme End Railway Station, now a tea shop and visitor centre at the start of the Manifold Way, takes you along quiet lanes on the ridge of the Manifold Valley and through the limestone village of Wetton. It then drops to the base of the valley, where it joins the Manifold Way to take in a glimpse of Thor's Cave before a welcome tea stop at Wetton Mill on the return run to Hulme End.

There are some steep climbs and descents and the ride includes public roads. Riders will need stamina, confidence and competence to cope with these demands, but the ride is within the reach of many family cyclists.

The Manifold Valley, steep-sided and beautiful, was carved out of the limestone plateau of the Peak District by the flow of the River Manifold. The river runs along its base, disappearing underground at times through the porous limestone of the riverbed. Open

and pastoral, with woodlands and limestone outcrops, the valley is a home for a wide vareity of wildlife. Red deer, foxes and badgers live in the wooded areas and it's possible to catch sight of stoats and weasels hunting for food along the dry limestone walls which border the valley's dairy and sheep farms.

Sheep and dairy farming have long been the staple of the valley – the Manifold River was once used for washing sheep – but arable farming has also left its mark. Wetton Mill, on the valley floor, was a riverside mill for grinding corn until it closed in the mid-19th century. And as you ride you may notice long field strips near Wetton. This has been the pattern for arable farming in the area since the medieval period.

You'll enjoy some enchanting views as you make your way along the valley ridge before heading towards the village of Wetton. There, close to the village green, is an 18th-century pub, which stands next to the parish church of St Margaret, built in the 14th century but damaged by fire in 1820. Much of the small church had to be rebuilt, but the church's original tower, which houses a remarkable six bells, survived. If you are feeling thirsty in Wetton, there is also a pleasant tea room in the village hall.

Clear the climb through the village and you'll find a welcome, but steep, descent to the Manifold Way at the base of the valley. Once there it's a short, flat ride along the Manifold Way for your view of Thor's Cave. And, after that, your return ride along the trail to Hulme End includes a  gentle but steady incline. The tea room at Wetton Mill is nearby and on your route. It's a delightful setting to stop and fortify yourself for the three-mile journey to the end of the ride.

THE BASICS

Distance: 8 miles / 13km

Gradient: Some steep climbs and descents, some undulation, the final 3½-mile return ride involves a gentle incline

Severity: Moderate

Approx. time: 2 hours

Terrain: Tarmac public roads, tarmac surface on cycle trail. Public roads have low levels of traffic. Manifold Way is mainly accessible only to cyclists and pedestrians, however, there is a short stretch open to cars and motorbikes subject to cycle and pedestrian priority

Maps: OS Explorer OL24 or OS Landranger 119

Start point: Hulme End Tea Junction (GR: SK 103593)

Parking: Adjacent to visitor centre (nearest postcode: SK17 0EZ)

Public toilets: Manifold Valley Visitor Centre, Wetton Mill

Nearest food: Hulme End Tea Junction at Manifold Valley Visitor Centre and at Wetton Mill

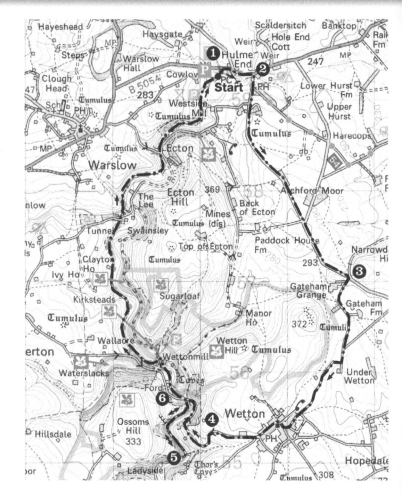

DIRECTIONS

1. Start at Manifold Valley Visitor Centre. Leave the centre and turn right onto the B5054.

2. After 0.3 miles on the B5054 turn right at the Manifold Inn heading in the direction of Alstonefield.
   Start a taxing 1-mile climb, after the crest continue for approximately 1 mile.

3. Turn right to Wetton approximately 1 mile.
   At the T-junction facing Ye Olde Royal Oake Pub'in Wetton turn right to start the 400-metre, steep climb through the village of Wetton.

4. Continue on the road as it forks left, following the signposted direction for Wetton Mill. You will pass Wetton Village Hall and the Old School tearooms on your left before you start your sharp descent to Wetton Mill.

5. At approximately 4 miles into your ride you reach a crossroads with the Manifold Way.
   Join the trail through the gate and head left for approximately half a mile to Thor's Cave, which can be reached by a climb up a footpath. (Remember to secure your bike if leaving it to visit the cave.)

6. After the cave it's an about-turn and head north for 3½ miles along the trail to Manifold Valley Visitor Centre.

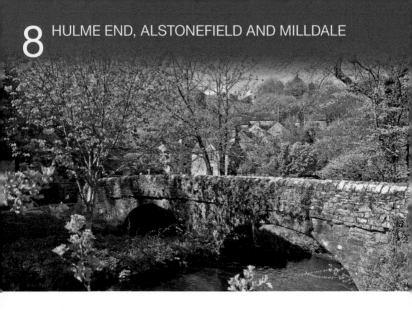

This nine-mile ride on quiet, public roads has plenty for family riders who are in the mood for a few challenges. You'll need the stamina to match some climbs, and to be competent on public roads and assured on descents. But if you like riding through rolling, sheep-farming countryside and steep-sided valleys, and exploring pretty villages and hamlets, you'll have a very enjoyable morning or afternoon's outing.

The ride ascends from Hulme End Tea Junction – a great start and end point for any ride with its excellent visitor centre and cafe – and moves quickly into the surrounding, rolling hills and sheep farms. Do the ride in spring and you'll have the cyclist's bonus of being able to glance over the hedgerows and dry limestone walls to see the spring lambs, watched over by their mothers as they find their first legs. Soft, rolling pastures give way to a more rugged landscape as you climb into the open hill country approaching Alstonefield.

Often missed by visitors to the area, Alstonefield is a pleasant and interesting village. Once on a busy packhorse route, it was mentioned in the 1086 Domesday Book, and was granted a market charter in 1308. Livestock markets were held here until the Victorian period and its days of commercial wealth can be seen in its impressive buildings, which spread from the village green. In the past there was a village pump, a reading room, a workhouse and a post office (sadly now closed).

Alstonefield's welcoming church, St Peter's, is also well worth a visit. Built mainly in the 16th century, it has some Norman elements and stands on a Saxon site. The Archbishop of York is recorded making a pastoral visit to a church here after a pagan uprising was quelled in 892, and Saxon crosses are preserved and set within the church porch.

From Alstonefield, it's a sharp descent to the entrance of the steep-sided and wooded valley leading to Milldale. You'll love this stretch of the ride – a mile-long saunter along the valley floor.

Milldale derives its name from the old corn mill that once stood here. It was demolished in the 19th century, but you can still see its remains and the old mill pond, where, as recently as the 1960s, shepherds washed their flocks before shearing. Nearby is the ancient packhorse bridge which spans the River Dove. The bridge features in the 17th-century book The Compleat Angler. Written by Izaak Walton, it recounts his conversations with his friend Charles Cotton. Isaak Walton features as 'Viator' (from the Latin for traveller), his friend as 'Pescator' (from the Latin for fisherman). The bridge is known as Viator's Bridge.

On the next stretch of your ride, provided you time your visit during trout fishing season, between March and October, you may well catch the timeless sight of fly fishing on the River Dove. Heading away from Milldale, this half-mile, pan-flat ride along the bank of the river passes a stretch of water revered by anglers. Your elevated position in the saddle gives you a view – unavailable to passing motorists – of the waterway, lightly shaded by woodland, passing over a series of weirs on its way to Dovedale. Enjoy the flat terrain while you can because at your first junction, you'll be turning sharp left into a one-mile beast of a climb back to Alstonefield.

Mercifully, the road levels before too long, and, although there's a climb as you leave the village, and some undulation as you retrace your route back to Hulme End, your final stages to Hulme End Tea Junction are pleasantly downhill.

THE BASICS

Distance: 9 miles / 14km
Gradient: Steep climbs and descents
Severity: Difficult
Approx. time: 2 to 2½ hours
Terrain: Quiet public roads
Maps: OS Explorer OL24 or OS Landranger 119
Start point: Hulme End Tea Junction (GR: SK 103593)
Parking: Adjacent to visitor centre (nearest postcode: SK17 0EZ)
Public toilets: Manifold Valley Visitor Centre, Hulme End Tea Junction, Alstonefield, Milldale
Nearest food: Hulme End Tea Junction, Alstonefield, Milldale

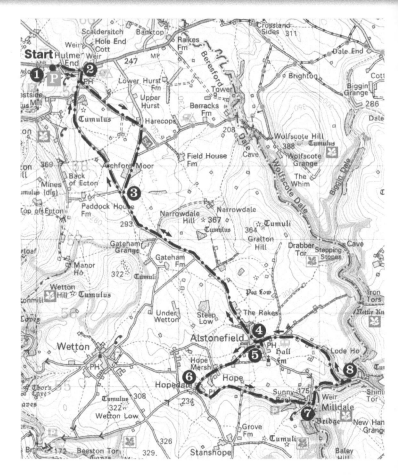

DIRECTIONS

1. Turning right (with the visitor centre to your right), join the B5054 from the exit of Hulme End Tea Junction.

2. After 300 metres turn right at the Manifold Inn. Turn left following sign for Cycle Route 549, continue for ¾ mile to junction. Turn right following signs for Alstonefield and Wetton, continue for approximately 1 mile.

3. At the T-junction turn left following sign for Alstonefield, continue for approximately 3 miles. Fork left into Alstonefield, passing toilets and small car park on your right.

4. Continue to junction, forking left into village. Take some time to wander around the village and perhaps enjoy, The George public house and St Peter's Church.

5. To continue your ride, with St Peter's and the village green behind you, turn left and left again towards Hopedale.

6. After ¾ mile / 1km, bear left, passing the Watts Russell Arms pub on your left. Continue for 1 mile to Milldale.

7. With Viator's Bridge behind you, ride for ½ mile to junction with Lode Lane.

8. Turn sharp left at junction, continue for 1 mile climb up to Alstonefield.

   Turn right at village green then continue past public toilets and car park to leave Alstonefield. Stay on this road for approximately 3 miles to Manifold Inn. Then turn left on to B5054 and in 300 metres turn left into Hulme End Tea Junction.

World Tour cycling races, like the Tour de France, always have a stage known as the 'Queen'. It often decides the outcome of days of competition and it's always tough. Well …. meet the 'Queen' of this collection!

Thirty miles long, it starts in historic Ilam, heads into wild moorland, embraces the Manifold Way and Tissington Trail, and returns, taking a steep descent, to Ilam. If you opt for this ride, you'll need a reasonable level of stamina and must be a competent bike handler. But if you are up to it you won't be disappointed.

Ilam is a fascinating village. For refreshments there's the Manifold Tea Room, which is owned by the National Trust and part of the Ilam Hall Estate that dominates the village. But there's more to Ilam than refreshments in a pleasant setting. It's a village rich in history.

Originally a Saxon settlement, much of the village was rebuilt in its peculiar alpine style in the 1820s by its then owner, Jesse Watts-Russell. He also erected the famous Ilam Cross as a monument to his beloved wife, Mary, who died, aged 48, in 1840. Bereft, he had the memorial designed on the model of the Eleanor Crosses, which were erected by Edward I to mark the resting places of his wife, Eleanor of Castile, on her final journey from Nottinghamshire to Westminster Abbey after her death in 1290.

Memories of tragedy and loss from an earlier period are also present in Ilam. St Bertram was a Saxon prince of Mercia who married a young wife in Ireland. Making their return journey to Mercia, his young princess gave birth and the family rested in the forest near Ilam. Tragedy struck when wolves fatally attacked his wife and child while Bertram was in the woods searching for food. Grief-stricken, he became a hermit and settled in Ilam. His remains are interred in St Bertram's Chapel, Ilam Church, a place of pilgrimage in the grounds of Ilam Hall.

Riding is hard as you leave Ilam behind and head north-west over the River Manifold for the first part of the steep climb to Throwley Moor. First respite comes when the road levels near the ruins of Throwley Hall. Built in 1603, it was lived in until 1877, when its occupants abandoned it for a new life in Australia. Amongst its earlier residents was Thomas, Baron Cromwell. He was a direct descendant of Thomas Cromwell, an architect of the English Reformation and subject of Hilary Mantel's historical novel Wolf Hall. The nearby farmhouse belongs to Throwley Hall Farm. A traditional beef farm, it raises sheep and Charolais cattle. You may see some as you ride alongside the farm's biers.

Pass the farm and you're on the steepest climb of the ride – the final push to Throwley Moor. You'll feel it, but on the moor things become easier. From there, you descend to Waterhouses to join the Manifold Way for a gentle pedal to Hulme End and from there to

the B5054 for a steady climb to Hartington, which at about mid-point on the ride, is great for a tea stop.

There's more steady but manageable climbing from Hartington to Hartington Signal Box, where you join the Tissington Trail for a welcome eight-mile gentle descent to Tissington. On the final leg of the ride you leave the Tissington Estate and cross the A515 to take a quiet road, with a gentle incline, to Thorpe. From Thorpe to llam things get exciting.

You'll first hit some undulation, including a couple of steep climbs. But clear this stretch and you've nothing but a steep drop between you and ride's end. It's a great descent. You'll be moving fast to llam Cross and the River Manifold winds like a silver ribbon beneath you. The one pity of this great ride is that you can't spend too much time looking at it!

THE BASICS

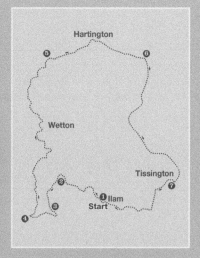

Distance: 30 miles / 48km

Gradient: Flat stretches, steep climbs and descents

Severity: Difficult

Approx. time: 4 hours

Terrain: Public road, well-surfaced trails

Maps: OS Explorer OL24 or OS Landranger 119

Start point: llam Cross, llam (GR: SK 134508)

Parking: llam, Moor Lane (free) or National Trust, llam Park (metered) (nearest postcode: DE6 2AZ)

Public toilets: National Trust, llam Park

Nearest food: Manifold Tea Room, National Trust llam Park, and cafes en route at Wetton Mill, Hulme End, Hartington and Tissington

DIRECTIONS

1. Starting at Ilam Cross, with the alpine cottages to your right and Ilam Hall Estate to your left, head north-east along Ilam Moor Lane towards Throwley Moor. After quarter of a mile of climbing turn left on to Lodge Lane for Throwley Hall.

   Stay on Lodge Lane as it forks slightly left. At Rushley Farm turn sharp right and begin a steep climb to Throwley Hall.

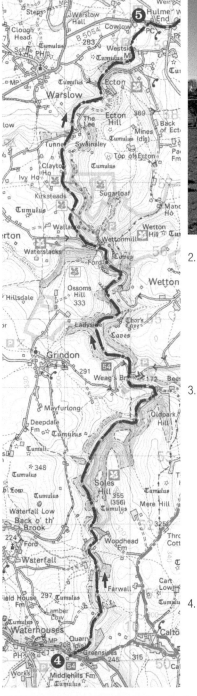

2. Pass Throwley Hall to the right and continue through the farmyard for Throwley Hall Farm (yes you can). Immediately after the farm buildings turn sharp left for Calton. You face a steep climb to Throwley Moor. On the moor begin your descent to Calton.

3. After approximately 1 mile of descent you meet a T-junction. Turn left (not signposted) heading for Calton. After ¼ mile of undulation you will meet a crossroads. Turn right signposted 1½ miles for Waterhouses. Continue to junction with A523; turn right with care.

   After approximately 200 metres join cycle lane on left for 200 metres until the road sign for Waterhouses.

4. Immediately to your right is the entrance to the Manifold Way, this 8 mile /13km trail will take you to Hulme End Tea Junction.

5. Leave Hulme End Tea Junction, turning right to join B5054 for 1½ miles to Hartington pass through Hartington on the B5054 turn right onto Hall Bank (it changes to High Cross) follow uphill for 500mts and bear right onto Highfield Lane and follow for 1 mile, at the junction bear right and then follow the road though Biggin for 1 mile until you come to an over bridge on the Tissington Trail. Take the ramp on the left hand side to join the trail and head south to Tissington.

6. Follow Tissington Trail for approximately 8 miles to Tissington village, leave the trail via the car park and take time to enjoy Tissington and a brief cup of tea.

7. Then pick up 'The Avenue' out of the Tissington Estate to the A515 junction, cross over, with care, onto Washbrook Lane.

   Continue on Washbrook Lane/Narlow Lane until junction with Spend Lane at The Old Dog pub. Cross Spend Lane and, passing the Old Dog on your left, follow Wintercroft Lane to Thorpe.

   From Thorpe continue approximately 1½ miles to Ilam (taking care on the descent).

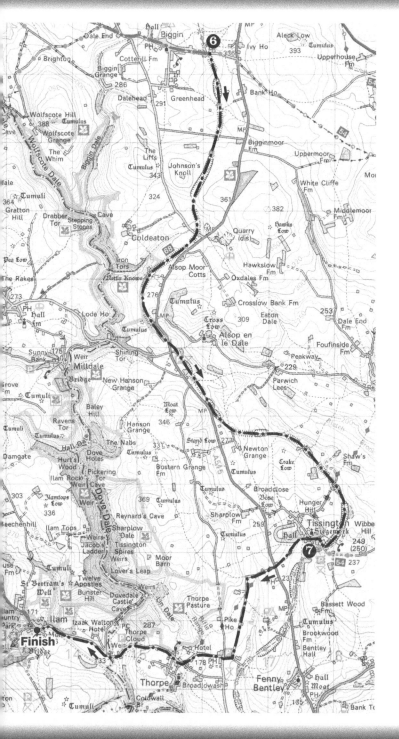

This short, intensive ride is ideal for family riders who may want to add a little strenuous exercise to a family day out on the nearby Tissington or Manifold Trails. It covers only seven miles, but they are seven miles with attitude!

There's plenty of climbing and the grand finale is a 10% descent from Thorpe to Ilam. And, for those who are interested in English history, there's an extra-special and little-known treat. Family riders will need an appetite for climbing and must be competent and confident bike handlers who are assured on rapid descents.

The ride starts amid the alpine-style cottages built by Ilam's 19th-century owner, Jesse Watts-Russell, who also erected the historic Ilam Cross in 1840 as a memorial to his

wife. Leaving the centre of Ilam, you cross the River Manifold and your hard work soon starts with the one-mile climb towards the tiny hamlet of Blore. A concentrated climb, it rises rapidly over Ilam and very quickly gives a panoramic view across the Manifold Valley towards Bunster Hill. Isolated limestone hills like Bunster are known as reef knolls. Not particularly high, at 329 metres (1,079 feet), its isolation gives it a dramatic prominence. You'll be able to enjoy it if you stop to look across the valley. Like Ilam Hall Estate, now lying beneath you, Bunster Hill, is owned by the National Trust.

The beautiful and peaceful little church of St Bartholomew, Blore Ray is at the top of the climb. With its out-of-the-way location and its historic architecture – built around 1100, it includes Norman work in the nave and a 14th-century tower and chancel – it's a perfect example of an English country church. Fragments of medieval painted glass illustrate the arms of local families as well as St Anne teaching the Blessed Virgin. England's turbulent history is here as well. There's a dismantled 14th-century stoup on the porch, a divided stone altar and a decapitated 15th-century brass memorial – all evidence of vandalism during the English Reformation.

And those with an interest in the history of the English Royal Family will be fascinated by the beautifully preserved 17th-century alabaster memorial to the local Bassett family of Blore Hall – direct ancestors of Queen Elizabeth II.

Riding on – and leaving Blore's window into English history behind you – you make a fast, two-mile descent of Yerley Hill to Mapleton. From here you are in for some undulation, which includes some stiff but short climbs on the two-mile ride to Thorpe. From Thorpe, it's a short 1½ miles to Ilam. You'll clear a couple of climbs and then it's the 10% drop to Ilam. This is a fairly straightforward descent with a small number of fairly gentle bends. It's fast and, with snatched glimpses of Ilam and the Manifold River beneath you, very memorable, but take care and keep your eyes on the road!

THE BASICS

Distance: 7 miles / 11km

Gradient: Steep climbs and descents

Severity: Difficult

Approx. time: 1½ to 2 hours

Terrain: Quiet public roads

Maps: OS Explorer OL24 & Explorer 259 or OS Landranger 119

Start point: Ilam Cross, Ilam (GR: SK 134508)

Parking: Ilam, Moor Lane (free), National Trust, Ilam Park (metered) (nearest postcode: DE6 2AZ)

Public toilets: National Trust, Ilam Park

Nearest food: Manifold Tea Room

St Bartholomew's Church

DIRECTIONS

1. Starting in Ilam Moor Lane with the alpine cottages and the Ilam Cross to your left and the Giles Gilbert Scott red telephone box to your right, take the road right to cross the bridge over the River Manifold. Continue on Ilam Moor Lane as you make the stiff, 1-mile climb to Blore. At the top of the hill continue over the crossroads to to visit St Bartholomew's Church.

2. Leaving the church behind you, facing towards Ilam, turn right to make the 2½ mile descent of Yerley Hill to Mapleton.

3. At the T-junction at Mapleton turn left towards Hinchley Wood and Thorpe.

4. After ½ mile turn left at the T-junction with Spend Lane.
Follow Spend Lane for 1½ miles to the Old Dog pub and turn left to join Wintercroft Lane.

5. From Thorpe continue for approximately 1½ miles to Ilam (taking care on descent).

Like its not-too-distant neighbour in the Sett Valley, the Longdendale Trail is one of the less well-known family rides in the Peak District. And, like its neighbour, it's none the worse for that.

Not as busy at peak times as some other trails, the Longdendale provides a great cycling route through one of the Dark Peak's most rugged and wild valleys. Once part of the trackbed for the former Manchester to Sheffield Railway, which linked the west of the country with the east, the trail runs between the pleasant town of Hadfield (which has cult status as the setting for the fictional 'Royston Vasey' in the darkly comic television series The League of Gentlemen) to the mouths of the famous, or possibly, infamous, Woodhead railway tunnels.

The trail rises gradually and manageably, as it runs along the Longdendale Valley. From gentle woodland, near Hadfield, to open moorland, near Woodhead, it covers just over 6.5 miles and gives great views of the Woodhead, Torside and Rhodeswood reservoirs. Built in the mid-19th century, they harness the River Etherow for the water supply to Manchester and Salford. This is a great ride over a good, hard-packed gravel surface. It's suitable for all family members, particularly those who like their countryside a little on the rugged side, and it's probably best undertaken in fine weather.

Steam trains once roared their way along this wild and sometimes windswept valley as they made their way across the country, emerging from, or heading to, the Woodhead railway tunnels, which for many years shaped the life of the valley. The first two of the three tunnels, which burrow for three miles through the Pennines to link the cities of Manchester and Sheffield, were built in the mid-19th century. Sixty men were killed in their construction and, at the time, it was said that soldiers fighting at the Battle of Waterloo had better hopes of survival than navvies working at Woodhead.

At their peak as many as eighty engines each day, many pulling goods wagons loaded with coal from the Yorkshire coalfields, rattled through the Victorian tunnels. But such a workload took its toll on their fabric, and the third tunnel was built in 1954 as their replacement. The entrances to all three, long closed to rail traffic, can now be reached by bike just beyond the site of the former castellated and once princely Woodhead Station, at the eastern tip of the Longdendale Trail.

The railway line closed completely in 1981 and, as time passed, where once there had been steam, power and noise came wildlife and nature. Opened as the Longdendale Trail in 1992, the route is owned and managed by United Utilities, for whom the valley's native wildlife is a high priority. You may well catch sight of foxes and hares on the moors and flycatchers and Canada geese are amongst the birdlife in the wooded areas.

It's possible to make your start and end point either in the west, at Hadfield, or in the east, at the former Woodhead Station. Both have parking facilities. But probably the most enjoyable route is to make your start and end point at Upper Longdendale Valley Car Park, Torside. The car park is in a stunning setting above the Torside Reservoir and has ample parking and toilet facilities. It's also close to the mid-point of the trail, which means that you can break your family ride into two, roughly equal legs.

First, head down the valley to Hadfield and back. When you reach Torside on your return run you might well stop for refreshments – you'll need a flask and sandwiches as there are no refreshment facilities on the trail. Suitably sustained, make the ride up to Woodhead through the wilder, more open, upper reaches of the valley. You'll begin to feel the gradient as you pass Woodhead dam, but you'll be happy in the knowledge that your return ride from the tunnels is not too long and has an incline in your favour. The tradition, by the way, is to touch the mouth of the 1954 tunnel before you make your return.

THE BASICS

Distance: 13 miles / 21km
Gradient: Gentle upward incline heading east
Severity: Moderate
Approx. time: 2 to 3 hours
Terrain: Good, hard-packed gravel – route includes one road crossing
Maps: OS Explorer OL1 or OS Landranger 110 & 109
Start point: Upper Longdendale Valley Car Park, Torside (GR: SK 068983)
Parking: Upper Longdendale Valley Car Park, Torside (nearest postcode: SK13 1JF)
Public toilets: Longdendale Valley Car Park, Torside
Nearest food: Hadfield

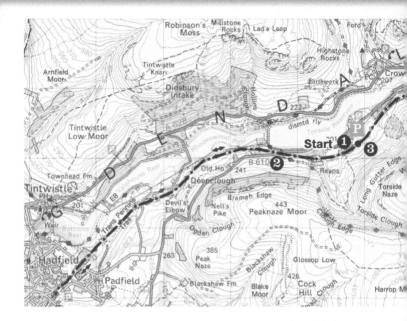

DIRECTIONS

(Start point at Upper Longdendale Valley
Car Park, Torside)

1. Join the trail at the gate from Torside
    Car Park. Turn right (with Torside
    Reservoir behind you) heading west
    towards Hadfield.

2. After approximately 1 mile you will need to cross the B6105, which can be busy,
    so approach with care.
    After crossing the B6105 rejoin and follow the trail westwards to Platt Street car
    park, Hadfield, which is your turning point.

3. After approximately 3½ miles from Hadfield watch for the gate (on your left) from
    the trail to Torside car park.
    After a break, rejoin the trail, this time turning left (with the reservoir behind you)
    heading east in the direction of Woodhead.
    Follow the trail for approximately 3 miles. It ends with a small gateway, which
    leads to the site of the former Woodhead Station and the Woodhead tunnels.

4. Turn and retrace your ride for approximately 3 miles to the gate to Torside Car
    Park.

This ride, an out-and-back, eighteen-mile trail along the Manifold Way, was once rated by the Guardian as amongst the best of Britain's bike rides. It's one of the easiest family rides in the Peak District on a very family-friendly cycle trail, which is blessed with a tarmac surface from start to finish and gradients gentle enough for even the smallest of legs. The Manifold Way is one of the area's family riding delights.

The trail runs along the bottom of the beautiful, steep-sided, limestone-edged Manifold Valley. For much of its length the trail borders the River Manifold, whose banks are rich in grasses and, in season, coloured by wild flowers. Adding magic to the ride, in summer the River Manifold disappears through its porous limestone bed after it passes Wetton Mill to resurface through a boil hole some miles south in historic Ilam Park.

The way was established in 1937 as a pedestrian path and is perhaps Britain's first example of a former railway line converted to leisure use. It was not officially opened to cyclists until 1981 (although limited stretches of the trail allow access to cars their speed is restricted and pedestrians and cyclists have priority).

Its former use was as the Leek and Manifold Light Railway, a narrow-gauge line (2' 6") which ran from Hulme End to Waterhouses. An imaginative project, it was also a commercial flop. Most of its ten halts were just that, and passengers had to clamber from small platforms up steep, unpaved paths to reach the nearest village.

Hulme End, one of the two termini, was the line's headquarters. It is now sympathetically restored as the Manifold Valley Visitor Centre and is the natural start and end point for the ride. There is a preserved section of the original line, a scale model of the original Hulme End station, information and leaflets about the trail and the surrounding area, and a first-class tea room.

Some family cyclists make the full eighteen-mile distance of the return trip from Hulme End to Waterhouses. But the trail climbs steadily, although not too steeply, from Thor's Cave to Waterhouses, and many with young children are content to cut the route short once they've seen the spectacular thirty-foot (10m) high, cavern, which towers above the trail on a limestone crag about four miles from Hulme End.

The magnificent, naturally formed cave can be reached from the trail by climbing a steep footpath. Human activity has been identified here as far back as the end of the Palaeolithic period 10,000 years ago and excavations have revealed stone tools, pottery, amber beads, bronze items and burial sites of at least seven people close by. Your first sight of it as you ride along the trail will definitely be one to savour.

Not quite so far back in time is Wetton Mill. It's a must for a visit, and possibly a cuppa, on your return leg. It closed as a water mill for grinding corn in 1857. Its remnants – two National Trust holiday cottages, limestone outhouses, the mill stream and pond, and the bridge over the river, erected by the 5th Duke of Devonshire in 1857 – make it an idyllic stop for leisure cyclists taking a breather before their three-mile, gentle return climb to Hulme End.

THE BASICS

Distance: 18 miles / 29km return

Gradient: Some steady inclines but mainly flat

Severity: Easy

Approx. time: 2 to 3 hours to Waterhouses and return
(2 hours to Wetton Mill and return)

Terrain: Tarmac cycle trail ideal for cycling. Some short stretches where there is access to cars but cyclists and pedestrians have priority

Maps: OS Explorer OL24 or OS Landranger 119

Start point: Manifold Valley Visitor Centre (GR: SK 103593)

Parking: Adjacent to visitor centre (nearest postcode: SK17 0EZ)

Public toilets: Manifold Valley Visitor Centre, Wetton Mill, Waterhouses Station

Nearest food: Hulme End Tea Junction, Wetton Mill

DIRECTIONS

1. Start at Manifold Valley Visitor Centre and follow the trail. You will travel through Swainsley Tunnel at approximately 1½ miles. Traffic other than cycles is allowed for a limited stretch at this point of the trail, but cyclists and pedestrians have priority.
   For approximately 3 miles the trail descends gently until it levels on its approach to Wetton Mill.
   Thor's Cave comes into sight at about 3½ miles from Hulme End.

2. The trail begins to ascend steadily, but not steeply, after Thor's Cave. It levels near its end on the outskirts of Waterhouses village, which is approximately 5½ miles from Thor's Cave.

3. Once you reach the outskirts of Waterhouses at the end point of the trail It's an about-turn for the return ride to your start point the Manifold Valley Visitor Centre.

ALTERNATIVE START AND FINISH POINT

It is possible to start at the southern end of the trail at what was once Waterhouses Station (GR: SK 085501; nearest postcode: ST10 3EG) and ride to Hulme End as a turning point. There are parking and toilet facilities there. To reach the Manifold Trail from the station you must descend a moderately steep tarmac ramp which drops down to the pavement on the busy A523 and then to the entrance to the Manifold Trail. Using Waterhouses as a start point has the advantage of close access to two cycle hire centres should you require cycle hire. These are Manifold Valley Cycle Hire, which is close to the old Waterhouses Station and Car Park, and Brown End Farm Cycle Hire, which is very close to the trail so you don't have to cross the busy A523.

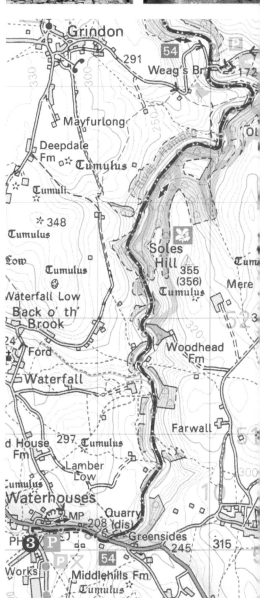

For some, the Monsal Trail is the most spectacular of all the Peak District's trails. Whether you agree is a matter of personal taste – all Peak District's trails have their special attractions. But, one thing is certain, running from Bakewell to Wye Dale, and providing 8¾ miles of traffic-free riding through the Derbyshire Dales, the Monsal Trail offers the the family cyclist a very rewarding outing.

Riding its long, winding tunnels, and crossing its magnificent viaduct, are experiences to remember. The surrounding scenery is a joy, and the trail's wide, well-surfaced track and gentle inclines make for easy riding on a great day out on the bike.

The trail, like most others in the Peak District, has been reclaimed for leisure use from the trackbed of a former railway line. Once the busy Midland Railway provided local transport and linked Derbyshire to the country's major cities. Opening in 1863, it closed on 1 July 1968, its end, like so many other branch lines, signalled in the 1963 Beeching Report. Happily, in 1981 the trail was opened, but only two of its tunnels, the shorter, Chee Tor No.2 and Rusher Cutting, were accessible. In 2011 the four longer tunnels were opened after an impressive £2.5 million restoration project, which was funded by the Department of Transport.

The longest of the tunnels are Headstone and Monsal Head at nearly 500 metres. Cressbrook and Litton are in the mid-400s, while Chee Tor No.1 is in the mid-300s. Cool, even on the hottest days, these long channels, cutting through the Derbyshire limestone, are cold enough in winter for icicles to form within them. A fascinating cycle ride into the past, with soot from countless steam engines still visible on their walls, they are literally lined with history.

The tunnels are lit constantly during daylight hours by 123 long-power, long-lasting fluorescent tubes, which, it's reassuring to know, are backed up with an emergency power supply. The lights are shut off at night and triggered in the morning by photocell sensors. When riding the tunnels during winter it's advisable to have bike lights as the tunnel lights may go out as the winter afternoon light fades.

Much of the surrounding countryside is screened by the attractive woodland which lines the trail. But there are plenty of opportunities to see the surrounding dales, not least when you ride over the Headstone Viaduct, which crosses Monsal Dale. This stunning piece of Victorian architecture, opened in 1863, is supported by five arches and measures over 90 metres (100 yards) across. Now a site of historical and architectural interest, its opening wasn't greeted with widespread approval. John Ruskin, the era's leading art critic, was horrified at its aesthetic impact. Protesting, he wrote. 'The valley is gone, and the gods with it.'

As with all of the Peak District trails, there are a number of start and finish points. It's possible to ride from Bakewell to Wye Dale and vice versa. But perhaps a more convenient pair of start and finish options are Wye Dale and Hassop Station. The return distance between these two destinations is just over 14 miles and both are very accessible with good parking, bike hire and refreshment facilities.

Hassop Station was built by the Midland Railway primarily for the benefit of the Duke of Devonshire, based at Chatsworth. Once called 'Hassop for Chatsworth', it boasted an elegant first-class waiting room. But although designed as a station for the aristocracy, it never fully achieved that aim. The dukes actually preferred Rowsley, another station along the line, and, without blue-blooded patronage, and serving such a thinly populated area, Hassop ultimately failed as a going concern for passengers. Serving its last passenger in 1942, it continued as a goods station until 1964 when it closed completely. Revived as an excellent trail start and end point, its first-class waiting room now does a very good job as a restaurant, complete with terrace overlooking the trail.

Whichever way you ride the trail, as long as you can manage a hike up a steep path and you have a bike lock to secure your bike, it will be worth leaving the trail to make the short but steep hike to Monsal Head. Accessible by the path, which is at the mouth, or exit, depending which way you ride, of the Headstone Tunnel, Monsal Head is one of the great locations of the Peak District. High above the trail, the view of the Headstone Viaduct, as it spans Monsal Dale, is breathtaking. And, if the climb up the path leaves you with little breath to take, there are refreshments close at hand at Hobb's Cafe.

THE BASICS

Distance: 9 miles / 14km
Gradient: Flat

Severity: Easy

Approx. time: 2 hours

Terrain: Well-surfaced cycle trail

Maps:OS Explorer OL 24 or OS Landranger 119

Start point: Wye Dale Car Park, Topley Pike (GR: SK 103724) or Hassop Station (GR: SK 218706)

Parking: Wye Dale Car Park, Topley Pike (nearest postcode: SK17 9TE) or Hassop Station car park (nearest postcode: DE45 1NW)

Public toilets: Millers Dale Station, Hassop Station

Nearest food: Basic snacks and refreshments at Blackwell Mill Cycle Hire; cafe and restaurant at Hassop Station

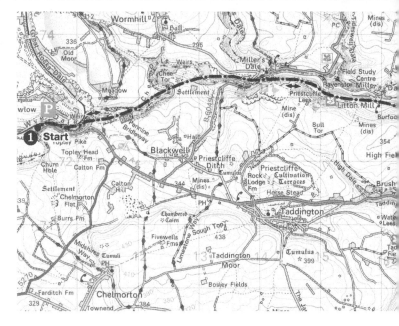

DIRECTIONS: WYE DALE TO HASSOP STATION

1. Take the bridleway (signposted as Bridleway to Monsal Trail) from Wye Dale car park to Wye Dale.

   After approximately ½ mile you'll see Blackwell Mill Cottages in front of you and you'll pass Blackwell Mill Cycle Hire on your right.

   Turn sharp right after Blackwell Mill Cycle Hire up a steep ramp that leads to the Monsal Trail.

   On joining the trail, head left towards Bakewell.

   Hassop Station is approximately 7 miles along the trail (exit left to station and well-earned refreshments).

   Return to Wye Dale.

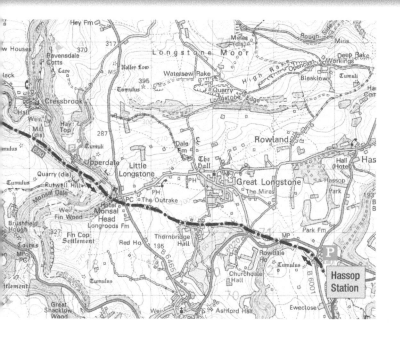

DIRECTIONS: HASSOP STATION TO WYE DALE

Join the trail at Hassop Station heading right towards Wye Dale.

After approximately 7 miles the trail ends at a signpost on the left and a gate leading to Wye Dale Exit. Follow ramp for Wye Dale and well-earned refreshments at Blackwell Mill Cycle Hire.

Return to Hassop Station.

Often missing from guide books, this easy five-mile out-and-back trail ride is one of the loveliest family rides in the Peak District. The trail follows the trackbed of the former railway line that linked the towns of Hayfield and New Mills to Manchester.

Once the busy line served the many mills and factories that were dotted throughout the valley and provided a rail link from Manchester for day-trippers to the Peak District. But when the British cotton industry declined so did the railway's business. It closed in 1970. Now the line is a well-surfaced trail for walkers, cyclists and horse riders, which follows the River Sett along the peaceful and scenic Sett Valley.

An ideal starting point is Hayfield Countryside Centre. The centre is now closed but there is a pleasant picnic area with parking and toilet facilities at the site. There is a

welcoming cafe at the former site of Birch Vale station about a mile along the ride. At the end of the trail is a footpath, which leads to Torrs Riverside Park, a site of historic interest and natural beauty. A trip to Sett Valley offers an easy ride and an excellent morning or afternoon outing for family cyclists.

Sett Valley is now a very different place from its days as an industrial and milling centre. At the height of the Industrial Revolution, the Sett and Goyt rivers were an ideal source of energy for cotton and paper mills, which in turn drew related industries like dye works into the valley. Now a pastoral setting for the trail, the valley sits peacefully beneath the more rugged hills of the Dark Peak such as nearby Kinder Scout and Lantern Pike, which lies across the river from the trail.

The 2½ mile ride from Hayfield to Torrs Riverside Park, where the Sett and Goyt rivers join to form an inspiring natural gorge, is lined with attractive woodland, but the trail still gives plenty of opportunity to see the surrounding countryside. A great way to learn about the history of the trail and the valley is through the 'Trail Tales' project. This imaginative oral history initiative, which was developed for Derbyshire County Council by Project eARTh and Hayfield Primary School, provides solar-powered audio units placed at vantage points and benches along the trail. Stop, take in the views, and press the units to hear a unique mix of music and spoken memories of the valley.

Another place to linger is Blue Bell Wood. This is a small patch of woodland immediately adjacent to the trail. It has lovely views across the valley to Lantern Pike, and, as its name suggests, is stocked with wild flowers including bluebells, flag iris and marsh marigolds. It's also a perfect home for birdlife and has its own colony of pipistrelle bats.

The route is undulating at times and has one short stretch where it may be easier for some young riders to push their bikes. But in the main it's an easy and safe ride that will be very attractive to parents with young children who are developing their cycling skills. It also has the advantage of being less well known than other trails, so even at weekends in summer it retains its tranquil atmosphere.

Be sure to bring a bike lock as the gorge at Torrs Riverside Park is reached at the end of the trail by way of a footpath. The short walk is very worthwhile. When this part of the north-west was the world's leader in cotton production, the combined power of the Goyt and Sett rivers as a source of energy made the gorge a hive of industry. Now, returned to its natural beauty, it's a wonderful turning point for a family ride.

THE BASICS

Distance: 5 miles / 8km
Gradient: Flat
Severity: Easy
Approx. time: 2 hours
Terrain: Well-surfaced cycle trail
Maps: OS ExplorerOL1 or OS Landranger 110
Start point: Hayfield Countryside Centre (GR: SK 036868)
Parking: Hayfield Countryside Centre car park (nearest postcode: SK22 2ES)
Public toilets: Hayfield Countryside Centre
Nearest food: Sett Valley Cafe, Birch Vale

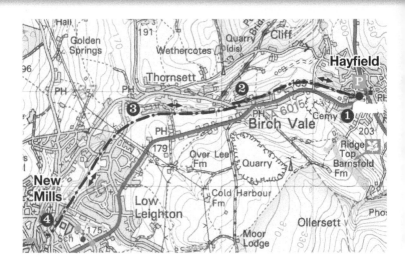

DIRECTIONS

1. Join the trail at its entrance at Hayfield Countryside Centre.

2. Following the trail there is a short, steep slope at approximately 1 mile where the trail crosses a quiet road. Cross the road and continue along the trail.

3. At approximately 2 miles the trail crosses another quiet road.

4. The trail finishes at approximately 2½ miles at a gate before a road crossing. Take the gate and cross the road to the footpath to Torrs Riverside Park. Find an opportunity to lock your bike and descend the steps to the gorge.

5. After exploring the gorge and its spectacular walkways, retrace your route back to Hayfield Countryside Centre.

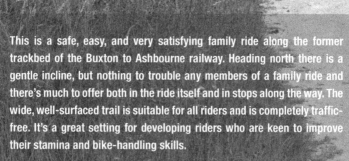

This is a safe, easy, and very satisfying family ride along the former trackbed of the Buxton to Ashbourne railway. Heading north there is a gentle incline, but nothing to trouble any members of a family ride and there's much to offer both in the ride itself and in stops along the way. The wide, well-surfaced trail is suitable for all riders and is completely traffic-free. It's a great setting for developing riders who are keen to improve their stamina and bike-handling skills.

Riding the Tissington Trail it's hard not to think of the lost age of British steam railway travel. At one time trains from Manchester to London used to rattle through the line's sleepy stations, where local dairy farmers loaded churns on to the milk train to London for the morning doorsteps of London's Finsbury Park.

All that ended as part of the transport restructuring that followed the 1963 Beeching Report. The line, sadly, like many other branch lines, closed, but what followed was an imaginative decision to convert the trackbed to leisure use for cyclists and pedestrians. Now it's one of the most popular leisure cycle rides in the Peak District.

Running thirteen miles from Ashbourne to Parsley Hay, the trail is wide, well surfaced on crushed limestone, and flat – an ideal ride for family cyclists. You don't, of course, have to sign up to a full, 26-mile, return ride of the trail. The sites of its former stations now provide car parks and toilets and an excellent choice of start and finish points along the way.

The village of Tissington is a particularly good one. From there you can take the trail over a twenty-mile return ride to Parsley Hay Cycle Hire Centre and Cafe – always being able to build in the option of stopping and turning at points along the way. There is parking space at the site of old Tissington station and Tissington itself is a charming village with a well-kept green, a pond, a tearoom, and a parish church with a buttressed Norman tower. Tissington Hall, at the heart of the village, dates back to Jacobean times as the home of Tissington Estate's longstanding owners, the FitzHerbert family.

Along the trail you'll pass peaceful pastures and cut through the dramatic limestone gorges that were hewn by 19th-century railway navvies. As you climb gently and the trail becomes raised on an embankment you'll have excellent views over rolling hills near Parsley Hay.

If the full 13 miles seems a long way for the first half of the ride, don't despair. Parsley Hay Cycle Hire Centre and Cafe is a friendly, thriving set-up at the edge of the trail. It's ideal for an ice cream and tea stop – enough to replenish any sagging energy levels, particularly since you've a gentle descent to look forward to as you return to your starting point.

ASHBOURNE CYCLE HIRE						
3.9	**THORPE CAR PARK**					
6.2	2.3	**TISSINGTON CAR PARK**				
10.6	6.7	4.4	**ALSOP EN LE DALE STATION CAR PARK**			
15.6	11.7	9.4	5.0	**BIGGIN**		
18.2	14.3	12.0	7.6	2.6	**HARTINGTON SIGNAL BOX CAR PARK**	
21.2	17.3	15.0	10.6	5.6	3	**PARSLEY HAY CYCLE HIRE**

If you want to jump on and off the Tissington Trail at different points, this chart will help you calculate the distance in km.

THE BASICS

Distance: Total return 23 miles / 42km

Gradient: A steady and gentle incline from the south

Severity: Easy

Approx. time: 2 to 3 hours

Terrain: Well-surfaced with crushed limestone, ideal for cycling

Maps: OS Explorer OL 24 or OS Landranger 119

Start point: Tissington Station (GR: SK 177520) or Parsley Hay (SK146637)

Parking: Adjacent to trail at start point, parking charges apply (nearest postcode: DE6 1RA)

Public toilets: Tissington Station, Parsley Hay Cycle Hire Centre

Nearest food: Tissington village and Parsley Hay Cycle Hire Centre

DIRECTIONS

Simple navigation – Select a starting point and pick up the trail heading either north or south. For an idea of distances (in km) from location to location refer to the chart on p.77.

CYCLE HIRE CENTRES

Ashbourne (☎ 01335 343156) to the north of the town centre on the Tissington Trail, just off the road to Mapleton.

Parsley Hay (☎ 01298 84493) at the junction of the High Peak and Tissington Trails, off the A515 Ashbourne to Buxton road.

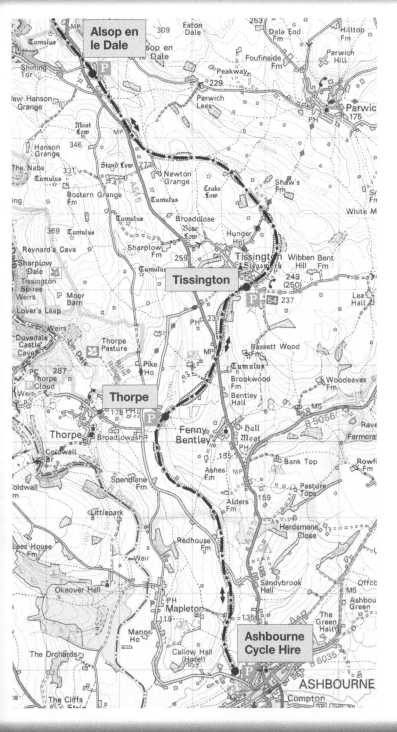

Carsington Water (iStock)

16 TISSINGTON, BRADBOURNE AND CARSINGTON WATER

This nine and a half mile ride which includes a mixture of open pasture and pleasant villages, partially follows the path of National Cycle Route 547. It is an undulating route along quiet lanes and off-road cycle trails. Although riders will need to be competent on public roads and have the stamina to cope with a twenty-mile, undulating ride, this is still a very manageable outing for family cyclists.

It starts in the historic village of Tissington, takes you through the open pasture of the Tissington Estate, makes a ford crossing of Bradbourne Brook, goes on to the interesting village of Bradbourne, and then makes Carsington Water Visitor Centre a refreshment break and turning point before your return ride.

Tissington village is an excellent starting point. Parking and toilet facilities are good and the Herbert's Fine English Tearooms are a fine refreshment venue. And there's also plenty to explore both before and after your ride. The Jacobean hall of the FitzHerbert family, estate owners for over 400 years,

is overlooked by the Norman tower of the church of St Mary. At the heart of the village, St Mary's Church is thought to be the source of the ancient practice of well-dressing – decorating wells with crafted flower displays, usually on a Christian religious theme. The legend is that, during the 14th century, Tissington escaped the Black Death as it ravaged England. This was, it is said, because Tissington's inhabitants drank only pure water from the village's wells. According to the legend, in each Ascension Week since, villagers have dressed and blessed the wells to give thanksgiving for the lucky escape of their ascendants. But it's also possible, that, like many festive traditions adopted by the Christian Church, well-dressing has its origins in pagan times. Many dressings in the villages of the Peak District have a 'well-queen', suggesting a link with ancient spring fertility rites.

The next village on this ride has no historical uncertainty over the origins of its special expression of thanksgiving. Bradbourne is a 'Thankful Village'. The journalist and writer Arthur Mee first used this term in his 1930s guide to the counties of England to describe those few villages to survive the Great War without the loss of any their young men. Of the 16,000 English villages recorded by Mee, he estimated that only 31 could call themselves 'Thankful'. (Further research has identified a total of 41 in England and Wales.) 'Thankful' villages normally have a plaque or a monument recording their gratitude and you'll see Bradbourne's as you pass through.

Your final stopping point is Carsington Water, the country's ninth biggest reservoir. Its pleasant shoreline, excellent views of the lake and surrounding countryside, and its first-rate cafe and visitor centre make this a perfect refreshment stop before your return ride to Tissington. And, for good measure, if any members of your party are feeling energetic, there is always the option of building in the Carsington Water ride as part of your trip, before your return to Tissington.

THE BASICS

Distance: 9½ miles / 14km

Gradient: Undulating throughout

Severity: Moderate

Approx. time: 2 to 3 hours

Terrain: Quiet public lanes on tarmac road surface and off-road cycle path

Maps: OS Explorer OL 24 or OS Landranger 119

Start point: The duck pond, The Green, Tissington village (GR: SK 176522)

Parking: Tissington Station (Nearest Postcode: DE6 1RA)

Public toilets: Tissington Station, Carsington Water Visitor Centre

Nearest food: Tissington village, Carsington Water Visitor Centre

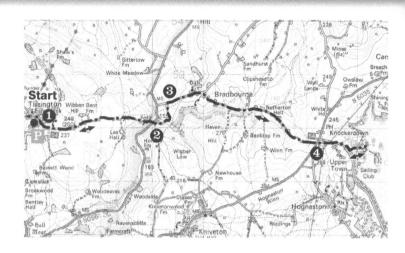

DIRECTIONS

1. Starting from the duck pond in Tissington village head east along The Green.
   After about 500 metres turn right onto Darfield Lane which becomes Brent
   Lane.
   Continue for approximately 1 mile until your descent to Bradbourne Brook at
   Tissington Ford. At the ford dismount to take the footpath and footbridge over
   the ford and then make the very short climb to the junction of the B5056.

2. As you look from the junction you will see, slightly to your right, the gated entrance to a field. This marks the continuation of Cycle Route 547, which is signposted at the gate. Follow this route through the field for approximately 750 metres until you meet Mill Lane. Clear the gate from the field and turn right onto Mill Lane.

3. Stay on Mill Lane until you enter Bradbourne in approximately ½ mile. You'll see the plaque to Bradbourne's Thankful Village status on the village cross. Heading south-west turn left onto Brackendale Lane until you meet a T-junction with the B5035.

4. Opposite you is the entrance to Big Lane; cross the B5035 and join Big Lane. Stay on Big Lane for approximately 500 metres.
    As Big Lane bends to the left, you will see the off-road continuation of Cycle Route 547 marked in front of you.
    Continue straight on along Route 547, which at this point is a cycle path.
    Stay on the path until the approach road to Carsington Visitor Centre, which you will see in front of you. Take time to explore the Carsington Water Visitor Centre and contemplate a circuit of the reservoir. See details on page 14

    Alternatively retrace your route to Tissington.

This straightforward twenty-mile ride is ideal if you are keen to branch out from the very safe environment of the trails and give some low-traffic lanes and a bit of distance riding a try. It starts and finishes on the Tissington Trail, but includes a stretch of steady riding on quiet, picturesque, lanes.

True, it does have a couple of climbs, which may test the energy of young, or even older, riders. But, as with most climbs in this book, they are neither too long, nor too steep, to be beyond a short period off the bike to wheel your way to the top if need be. Riders must be competent on public roads to take on this route.

Essentially a trail ride, which includes a slightly more taxing and adventurous detour, your start is the old Tissington station, which borders the Tissington Trail. Supplied with car parking and toilet facilities, the site also has an interesting picture of the station in its heyday on the car park information board. Incidentally, if you haven't already explored the village itself, make sure that you do, either at the start or end of your ride – you won't be disappointed.

Heading north-east from Tissington to Parsley Hay, your first views of the surrounding countryside are glimpsed through gaps in the trees that line the trail. But as the trail gently climbs, it clears the trees and gives impressive views to the west of tree-topped knolls and rolling countryside.

Along the trail is Parsley Hay Cycle Hire Centre and Cafe, which is a natural turning point and an excellent place for your mid-ride refreshments. From there, it's about-turn until you reach the landmark Hartington Station Signal Box. It's here that you part company from the trail to go and experience, at closer quarters, the countryside that you have been viewing from the vantage point of the trail.

Ahead is a four-mile route into the countryside, which includes a bit of hill-climbing before you rejoin the Tissington Trail at one of the embankments that you rode over on your outbound ride. Once there, the toughest stage is over and it's a gentle descent along the trail back to Tissington.

Approximately twenty miles in all, and including some hill-climbing on country lanes, this will be a slightly challenging and very satisfying ride for the developing family cyclist. Your refreshments at Tissington village will be more than welcome at the end of the ride.

THE BASICS

Distance: 20 miles / 32km

Gradient: Gentle inclines on Tissington Trail, with steady climbs and descents on road sections

Severity: Moderate

Approx. time: 2 to 3 hours

Terrain: Public, quiet lanes on tarmac road surface and well-surfaced cycle trail

Maps: OS Explorer OL 24 or OS Landranger 119

Start point: Tissington Station car park (GR: SK 177520)

Parking: Tissington Station car park (nearest postcode: DE6 1RA)

Public toilets: Tissington Station, Parsley Hay Cycle Hire Centre and Cafe

Nearest food: Tissington village, Parsley Hay Cycle Hire Centre and Cafe

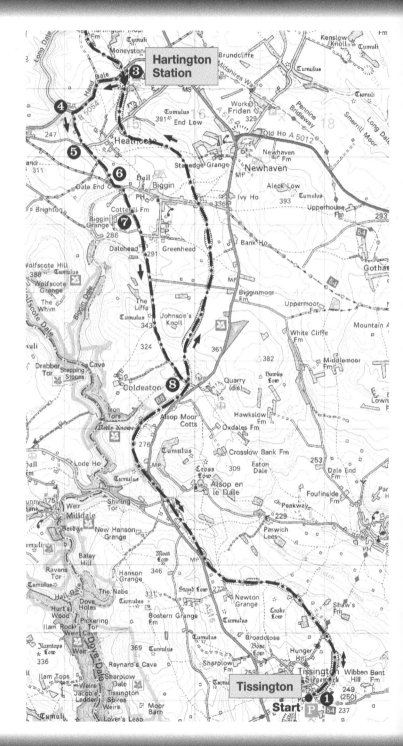

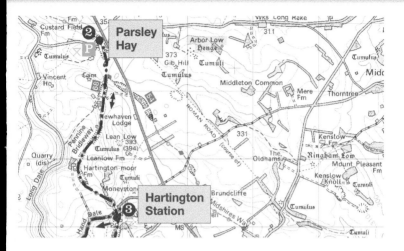

DIRECTIONS

1. Starting from Tissington Station car park, join the Tissington Trail and head approximately 10 miles north-east to Parsley Hay Cycle Hire Centre and Cafe.

2. Refreshed, make an about-turn and retrace your ride for approximately 3 miles to Hartington Signal Box and Station.

3. Leave the trail and, turning left, join the B5054, heading in the direction of Hartington.

4. After approximately 1 mile of steady descent turn sharp left onto Harding's Lane in the direction of High Cross.

5. Make the steady climb up Harding's Lane. After about half a mile you will pass a duck pond on your left with High Cross to your right. Continue on Harding's Lane in the direction of Biggin.

6. After approximately 1 mile you will meet a fork in the road. To the left, heading in the direction of Biggin, is Main Street. Slightly to the right is Liff's Road. Take the slight right turn and join Liff's Road.

6. Continue on Liff's Road for approximately 2½ miles. This will involve a steady climb followed by a pleasant descent as you approach the Tissington Trail embankment, which you will see in front of you on your descent.

8. At the embankment dismount and take the narrow grassy path up the embankment to Tissington Trail. Retrace your outward ride along the Tissington Trail with a gentle 4-mile return descent to your start point at Tissington Station.

This short ride, just eight and a half miles in all, is ideal as an adventurous addition to a day out on the Monsal Trail. The ride has easy and steady stretches on the trail but makes a detour, which includes a steep descent into beautiful Millers Dale, and an equally steep climb up a footpath to rejoin the Monsal Trail. You'll need both stamina and bike-handling competence for this ride, but, if you are able, your trip into Millers Dale makes it well worth the effort.

The ride starts in the peaceful and picturesque setting of Wye Dale before a short ride along the Monsal Trail to Millers Dale Station. In the heyday of the former Manchester, Buxton, Matlock and Midland Junction Railway, Millers Dale was an important junction. Here passengers for Buxton joined or left the line for connections to the cities of Manchester and London. That all ended when the line closed in 1968 and now it's a quiet stop for cyclists and pedestrians on the Monsal Trail. The station's toilets and its strategically positioned ice cream van are now its most important features.

It's at Millers Dale Station that you leave the trail for your short but well worthwhile adventure ride. You'll make a steep descent from the trail to pass under two of the trail's magnificent viaducts. The first of these majestic twin wrought-iron superstructures was built by the Midland Railway in 1866. The second, which now carries the trail, was added in 1905 to cope with increasing demand for both passenger and goods traffic on the once

busy railway line. From there, you make your way towards Litton Mill along a quiet lane, which borders the River Wye as it winds through the scenic gorge of Millers Dale. Millers Dale is one of the less visited locations in the area and you'll be able to stop and enjoy its tranquillity as you wind your way along the river bank. The landmark for your turning point and route back to the Monsal Trail, which is by way of a narrow wooden bridge over the river, is Ravenstor.

Ravenstor is a dramatic overhanging limestone cliff, which has become a major destination for British climbers. Stop to look at the cliff and you'll see the residue of the chalk which they use to help keep their hands dry when they edge their way by their fingertips up this imposing rock face.

A short way downstream from your turning point is Litton Mill. This is a small hamlet, which was built around a former cotton mill that was burned down in 1897. The former mill holds an unenviable place in 19th-century British social history. Its owners were exposed for their cruel misuse of orphans who were sent, under Poor Law provisions, from the country's rapidly expanding cities to be indentured as apprentices at factories and mills. Many apprentices at Litton Mill, as in other locations, did not survive into adulthood. One who did was Robert Blincoe. He made an exposé of his scandalous treatment at Litton Mill and public outrage shaped the passage of the first Factories Act in 1833.

Once over the River Wye, by way of the wooden bridge, it's up the steep path to the Monsal Trail, which sits above you. From there you'll head back along the trail, through Millers Dale Station and Chee Dale Tunnels, to Wyedale for refreshment at the friendly and welcoming 'Tuck Shop' at Blackwell Mill Cycle Hire.

THE BASICS

Distance: 8½ miles / 14km

Gradient: Flat stretches on Monsal Trail, but ride includes a sharp descent on a public road and a steep ascent up steps on a public footpath where bikes will have to be carried or pushed

Severity: Moderate

Approx. time: 2 hours

Terrain: Well-surfaced cycle trail and tarmac lanes, including public roads

Maps: OS Explorer OL 24 or OS Landranger 119

Start point: Wye Dale Car Park, Topley Pike (GR: SK 103724)

Parking: Wye Dale Car Park, Topley Pike (nearest postcode: SK17 9TE)

Public toilets: Millers Dale Station

Nearest food: Basic snacks and refreshments at Blackwell Mill Cycle Hire

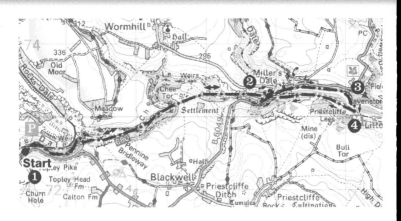

DIRECTIONS

1. Take the bridleway (signposted as Bridleway to Monsail Trail) from Wye Dale car park to Wye Dale.

   After approximately half a mile you'll see Blackwell Mill Cottages in front of you and pass Blackwell Mill Cycle Hire on your right.

   Turn sharp right after Blackwell Mill Cycle Hire up a steep ramp that leads to the Monsal Trail.

   On joining the trail, head left towards Bakewell.

2. After 1½ miles you reach Millers Dale Station.

    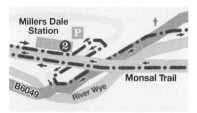

    On leaving the station you'll see a corrugated iron house called 'The Wriggly Tin' immediately in front of you. Turn sharp right and descend the hill with care. The road bends sharply and meets a T-junction with the B6049, which can carry some heavy traffic. Turn left, passing under the twin viaducts.

    After approximately half a mile on the B6049 you will see the small church of St Anne's on your left. This is almost opposite a fork in the road. Leave the B6049 and take the fork to the right, following the signpost, which marks a dead end at Litton Mill. You will pass the Angler's Rest pub.

3. Follow the lane until you see the cliff face of Ravenstor on your left. Just beyond the cliff on your right you'll see a signpost to a public footpath across the narrow wooden footbridge over the River Wye.

4. Cross the bridge and take the steep steps up to the Monsal Trail.

    Turn right towards Millers Dale Station, approximately 2½ miles along the trail.

    After Millers Dale Station continue for 1½ miles to the end of the trail

    at Wye Dale. Take the ramp from the trail to Blackwell Mill Cycle Hire. Pass Blackwell Mill Cycle Hire up the bridleway for ½ mile to Wye Dale car park.

I'm a writer and photographer who specialises in endurance sport. I've a long relationship with cycling, which started way back in the 1960s. Then, a greengrocer's order boy, I rode a big, old, green delivery bike. It would probably break a catalogue of safety regulations now, but I loved riding it. Since those days, I've ridden competitively as an amateur and covered many miles in Europe and the United States exploring trails and roads as a touring cyclist. A strong advocate of safe and enjoyable cycling, I'm truly hoping that this collection will help family riders to enjoy some great days out in a wonderful part of the world and inspire a love of cycling that will last for many years.